Nelson Handwriting

Developing Skills

RED LEVEL

Anita Warwick

Series editor: John Jackman

OXFORD
UNIVERSITY PRESS

CONTENTS/SCOPE AND SEQUENCE

Introduction and practice of the four handwriting joins.

Page	Focus	Extra	Extension	Focus resource	Extension resource
4-5 Unit 1 Holidays	practise the first join: un, um	bun, mum	match and copy captions	un, bun, gun, sun, nun trace and copy pattern and copy words	un, um, buns, nuns, hums, mums, sums trace and copy the first join, words and sentence
6-7 Unit 2 Holidays	practise the first join: ig, id	lid, dig	choose words and copy sentences	ig, big, pig, dig trace and copy pattern and copy words	ig, big, id, did, kid, lid, hid trace and copy the first join, words and sentence
8-9 Unit 3 Birthdays	practise the first join: ed, eg	bed, leg	punctuate and copy sentences	ed, bed, ted, le, led trace and copy pattern and copy words	Jed, eg, beg, peg, leg trace and copy the first join, words and sentence
10-11 Unit 4 Birthdays	practise the first join: an, ar	nan, car	choose words and copy sentences	an, can, man, nan, pan, tan trace and copy pattern and words	an, Nan, ar, car, tar, star trace and copy the first join, words and sentence
12-13 Unit 5 Food	practise the first join: ing, ung	rhyming ing, ung and ang words	copy sentence	ng, ing, ding, sing, ping, king trace and copy pattern and words	ung, lung, sung, ang, gang, sang trace and copy the first join, words and sentence
14-15 Unit 6 Food	practise the second join: ch, sh	chip, ship	write out menu order	ch, chip, child, chew, sh, ship, shed, shell trace and copy pattern and words	ch, chips, chimps, cheeky trace and copy second join, words and sentence
16-17 Unit 7 Foxes	practise the second join: th, tl	the, them	choose words and copy sentences	th, them, then, this, that, thank trace and copy pattern and words	the, think trace and copy second join, words and sentence
18-19 Unit 8 Foxes	practise the second join: ll, ill	ill, pill	choose words and copy sentences	ill, hill, mill, pill, bill, till trace and copy pattern and words	hill, Bill, Jill trace and copy second join, words and sentence
20-21 Unit 9 Beans	practise the second join: sli, slu	slid, slug	choose words and copy sentences	sl, slid, slide, slip, slippy, slipper trace and copy pattern and words	sl, slug, slugs, slush trace and copy second join, words and sentence
22-23 Unit 10 Beans	practise the second join: ck, ack	sack, back	choose words and copy sentences	ack, pack, ick, kick, eck, peck trace and copy pattern and words	ck, back, mack, sack trace and copy second join, words and sentence
24-25 Check-up 1	*Check-up*	*Check-up*	*Check-up*	*Check-up*	*Check-up*

age	Focus	Extra	Extension	Focus resource	Extension resource
6-27 it 11 oys	practise the second join: st, sti	still, stilts	choose words and copy sentences	st, stick, sticky, sticker, sting, stitch trace and copy pattern and words	st, still, stile, step, steep, stay, stall trace and copy words and sentence
8-29 nit 12 oys	practise the second join: ink, unk	pink, junk	choose words and copy sentences	nk, ink, pink, sink, link, blink trace and copy pattern and words	unk, bunk, punk, dunk, sunk trace and copy second join, words and sentence
0-31 nit 13 omes	practise the third join: od, og	dog, frog	choose words and copy sentences	og, cog, dog, log, fog, frog trace and copy pattern and words	nod, rod, log, frogs trace and copy words and sentence
2-33 nit 14 omes	practise the third join: re, ve	are, there	copy poem	re, read, reed, reel, real trace and copy pattern and words	re, red, ve, very, we, went trace and copy third join, words and sentence
4-35 nit 15 igers	practise the third join: oon, oom	moon, room	choose words and copy sentences	oo, soon, spoon, moon, room, broom, groom trace and copy pattern and words	oo, zoo, zoom, soon trace and copy third join, words and sentence
6-37 nit 16 igers	practise the fourth join: wl, vl	growl, prowl	copy acrostic poem	wl, bowl, slowly, crawl, trawl, trawler trace and copy pattern and words	howl, growl, prowl trace and copy words and sentence
8-39 nit 17 yself	practise the fourth join: of, ff	of, off	choose words and copy sentences	of, ff, uff, huff, puff, cuff, stuff trace and copy pattern and words	ff, of, off trace and copy pattern and words choose word and copy sentence
0-41 nit 18 yself	practise the fourth join: fl, flo	floor, flood	copy poem	fl, flo, float, flood, floor, flower trace and copy pattern and words	copy poem
-43 nit 19 njoined tters	practise the break letters: b, p, g, q, y, j, z	be, poke	copy poem and underline break letters	practise the break letters	copy phrases
-45 nit 20 njoined tters	practise capital letters	alphabetical ordering: children's names	alphabetical ordering: children's names	finish the patterns	copy classroom captions using capital letters
-48 heck-up 2	*Check-up*	*Check-up*	*Check-up*	*Check-up*	*Check-up*

Practising the first join.

Run, Mum. Run.

FOCUS

A Copy this pattern into your book.

ᴜᴜᴜ   ᴜᴜᴜ   ᴜᴜᴜ   ᴜᴜᴜ

B Copy these letters into your book.

un   un   un   un   un

um   um   um   um   um

Be careful!
Make sure you take
your pencil back up to
the top before you
start your next letter.

EXTRA

ake these words. Copy them into your book.

$$b + un = bun \quad bun \quad bun$$

$$m + um = mum \quad mum \quad mum$$

EXTENSION

atch a caption to each holiday snap and write them into your book.

Tip mum in.

Fun in a bun.

1

2

Practising the first join.

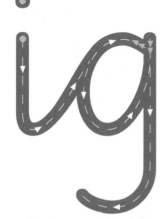

Dig, dig, dig.

 OCUS

A Copy this pattern into your book.

ununc ununc ununc ununc

B Copy these letters into your book.

ig ig ig ig ig
id id id id id

The letter g has
a descender.
Its tail goes below
the line.

 **XTRA**

Make these words. Copy them into your book.

l + id = lid   lid   lid

d + ig = dig   dig   dig

XTENSION

Look at the words in the box.

lid dig

Copy these sentences into your book.
Write in the missing words.

Tid hid in a big ____.
Dig, Kim, ____.

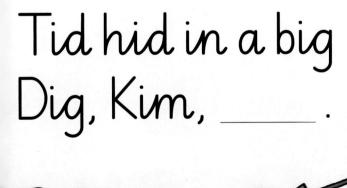

ed

Jed has a bed.

FOCUS

A Copy this pattern into your book.

llll llll llll llll

B Copy these letters into your book.

ed ed ed ed ed
eg eg eg eg eg

EXTRA

Make these words. Copy them into your book.

b + ed = bed   bed   bed

l + eg = leg   leg   leg

EXTENSION

Copy these sentences into your book.
Put in the missing capital letters and full stops.

ed has a new bed

ben has a bad leg

Be careful!
Capital letters do not
join.

Practising the first join.

an

I can go in my car.

ocus

A Copy this pattern into your book.

B Copy these letters into your book.

an an an an an

ar ar ar ar ar

Make these words. Copy them into your book.

n + an = nan   nan   nan

c + ar = car   car   car

Take care!
Make sure all these letters are the same height and size.

XTENSION

Look at the words in the box.

Nan   car

Copy the sentences into your book. Write in the missing words.

_____ has a nap.

Dad is in Ben's new _____.

Practising the first join.

ng

Sing, sing, sing.

FOCUS

A Copy this pattern into your book.

B Copy these letters into your book.

ing ing ing ing ing
ung ung ung ung ung

Copy the words below.
Write two words that rhyme.

Be careful!
The letter g has a
descender. Its tail
goes below the line.

ing	ung	ang
sing	hung	bang
ding		
king		

Copy this sentence into your book.

Ten sausages
in a pan go bang.

Practising the second join.

ch

ship and chips

FOCUS

A Copy this pattern into your book.

cd cd cd cd cd cd cd

B Copy these letters into your book.

ch ch ch ch ch
sh sh sh sh sh

Make these words. Copy them into your book.

| ch + ip | = | chip | chip | chip |
| sh + ip | = | ship | ship | ship |

XTENSION

What would you choose to eat from the menu?
Write your order into your book.

The Ship and Chip Inn

Fish and chips	80p
Fish, chips and peas	95p
Chips and beans	65p
Chips in a bun in	
a big dish	60p

Practising the second join.

th

The cub and the cat hid.

 OCUS

A Copy this pattern into your book.

ⵡⵡ   ⵡⵡ   ⵡⵡ   ⵡⵡ

B Copy these letters into your book.

th th th th th
tl tl tl tl tl

EXTRA

Copy these words into your book.

the   the   the   the

them   them   them   them

Be careful!
The letter t is not as
tall as the letter h.

EXTENSION

Choose the right word. Write the sentences into your book.

I can see (the/them).
A little cub is eating
all (the/them) cakes.

Practising the second join.

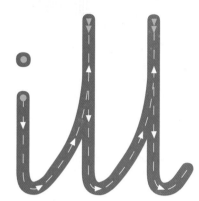

The cub is ill.

 OCUS

A Copy this pattern into your book.

lululululululululu

B Copy these letters into your book.

ll ll ll ll ll

ill ill ill ill ill

opy these words into your book.

ill ill ill ill

pill pill pill pill

Tall letters have **ascenders**. The letter l has an ascender.

ook at the words in the box.

| pill ill |

opy the sentences into your book. Write in the missing words.

A cub is ____.

A ____ made him better.

Practising the second join.

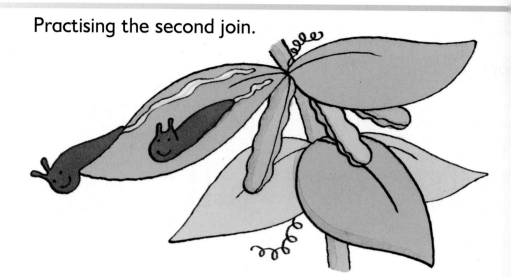

The slugs slid.

 **F**OCUS

A Copy this pattern into your book.

slsl   slsl   slsl   slsl

B Copy these letters into your book.

sli   sli   sli   sli   sli

slu   slu   slu   slu   slu

 **XTRA**

opy these words into your book.

slid slid slid slid

slug slug slug slug

Put the dot above the letter i after you have finished writing the word.

 **XTENSION**

hoose the right word from the box to fill the gaps.
opy the sentences into your book.

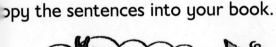

slug slid

A _____ ate the beans.

He _____ into the

giant's lap.

Practising the second join.

Quick, Jack. Get the sack.

OCUS

A Copy this pattern into your book.

ckck ckck ckck ckck

B Copy these letters into your book.

ck   ck   ck   ck   ck
ack ack ack ack ack

Make these words. Copy them into your book.

sa + ck = sack sack sack

ba + ck = back back back

b is a break letter.
It does not join to the
next letter.

Copy these sentences into your books.
Choose the right word to fill the gaps.

back
sack

Jack had a _____ on
his _____.

packed
sack

Jack made it. He _____
all the gems in his _____.

CHECK-UP 1

OCUS

Copy these patterns into your book.

  ʊʊ   ʊʊ   ʊʊ   ʊʊ

  ıcʊc   ıcʊc   ıcʊc   ıcʊc

  eee   eee   eee   eee

  ʊʊʟ   ʊʊʟ   ʊʊʟ   ʊʊʟ

  ckck   ckck   ckck   ckck

24

Copy these words into your book.

bun	mum	leg	bed
sing	chips	nan	car
slug	sack	back	ill

 **XTENSION**

Copy this sentence into your book.

Jack and Jill go up the hill.

Practising the second join.

Step up, step up to my stall.

A Copy this pattern into your book.

B Copy these letters into your book.

st   st   st   st   st
sti   sti   sti   sti   sti

 **XTRA**

Make these words. Copy them into your book.

st + ill = *still* *still* *still*

st + ilts = *stilts* *stilts* *stilts*

Take care!
Cross the letter t after
you have finished
writing the word.

XTENSION

Choose the right word. Write the sentences into your book.

Justin can see *(still/stilts)*.

Estelle thinks Santa is *(still/ sting)* inside.

27

Practising the second join.

nk

What is in the sink?

FOCUS

A Copy this pattern into your book.

nlnl nlnl nlnl nlnl

B Copy these letters into your book.

ink ink ink ink ink
unk unk unk unk unk

Make these words. Copy them into your book.

pi + nk = pink   pink   pink

ju + nk = junk   junk   junk

Be careful!
p and j are break letters.
They do not join to the next letter.

EXTENSION

Choose the right word to fill the gaps.
Copy the sentences into your book.

punk
junk
Mum said all the ___ had to go to the jumble sale.

sink
pink
Sita put her ___ pens in the sack.

Practising the third join.

The frog is on a log.

OCUS

A Copy this pattern into your book.

ooo ooo ooo ooo

B Copy these letters into your book.

od od od od od

og og og og og

Remember to keep your letters spaced correctly like this:

od

EXTRA

Make these words. Copy them into your book.

d + og = dog   dog   dog

fr + og = frog   frog   frog

EXTENSION

Choose the right word.
Copy the sentences into your book.

A (cat/dog) lives in a kennel.

A (bird/frog) lives in a pond.

Practising the third join.

There are people moving in.

OCUS

A Copy this pattern into your book.

rere rere rere rere

B Copy these letters into your book.

re re re re re

ve ve ve ve ve

Take care!
Bring your pencil down
to write the letter *e*,
like this:

re

 **XTRA**

opy these words in to your book.

are   are   are   are

there   there   there   there

XTENSION

opy this poem into your book.

Are there any apples
On your apple tree?
Do you think your mother
Will ask me in to tea?

from 'The New Neighbour' by Rose Fyleman

Practising the third join.

I can see the moon.

OCUS

A Copy this pattern into your book.

roro roro roro roro

B Copy these letters into your book.

oon oon oon oon oon

oom oom oom oom oom

Remember to keep your letters spaced correctly, like this:

 XTRA

opy these words in to your book.

moon   moon   moon   moon

room   room   room   room

XTENSION

hoose the correct word to finish the sentence.
opy the sentences into your book.

The tiger crept into
the (broom/room).
The (moon/soon) was
shining through the window.

Practising the fourth join.

He prowls in the dark.

 OCUS

A Copy this pattern into your book.

B Copy these letters into your book.

wl wl wl wl wl

vl vl vl vl vl

The join will help you
to leave the correct
space between your
letters, like this:

wl

Copy these words in to your book.

gr +owl = growl growl growl

pr +owl = prowl prowl prowl

EXTENSION

Copy this poem into your book.

Terrifyingly fierce

I glow through my stripes as I

Gracefully prowl at

Evening and night

Regard and admire me.

'Tiger Acrostic' by *John Cotton*

Practising the fourth join.

I like soft coffee toffees.

 OCUS

A Copy this pattern into your book.

fff   fff   fff   fff

B Copy these letters into your book.

of of of of of
ff ff ff ff ff

Be careful!
The join to the second
starts when you cross
the first f, like this:

f ff

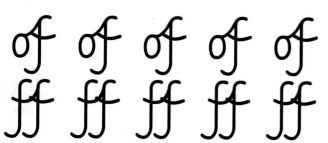

Copy these words into your book.

XTENSION

Choose of or off to finish these sentences.
Copy the sentences into your book.

I love the smell ____ daffodils.

Fluff falls ____ my jumper.

Practising the fourth join.

fl

Flip flop across the floor.

FOCUS

A Copy this pattern into your book.

lolo lolo lolo lolo

B Copy these letters into your book.

fl fl fl fl fl
flo flo flo flo flo

 XTRA

Copy these words in to your book.

floor   floor   floor

flood   flood   flood

Take care!
The letter f has a
straight back.

 XTENSION

Copy this poem into your book.

I lost my toothbrush
I slammed the door,
I dropped an egg
On the kitchen floor.

from 'The Wrong Start' by Marchette Chute

Practising the break letters.

Don't join a break letter.

OCUS

A Look at the break letters.

b p g q y j z

B Copy these break letters into your book.

bbb

ppp

ggg

qqq

yyy

jjj

zzz

EXTRA

Copy these words into your book.

be	be	be	be
poke	poke	poke	poke

EXTENSION

Copy this poem into your book.

If you should meet a crocodile,
Don't take a stick and poke him.
Ignore the welcome in his smile,
Be careful not to stroke him.

from *'If you should meet a crocodile'*, Anonymous

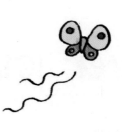

Underline all the break letters.

Practising capital letters.

Never join CAPITAL LETTERS

 OCUS

A Look at the capital letters.

A B C D E F G H I J K L M
N O P Q R S T U V W X Y Z

B Write each capital letter three times in your book.
The first one is done to help you.

AAA

ABCDEFGHIJKLM
NOPQRSTUVWXYZ

Remember,
capital letters are the
same height as
ascenders.

44

 **XTRA**

Look at the pictures and names of 12 children in Ben's class.
Copy their names in alphabetical order.

Jalila

Adam

Dan

Ben

Emma

Grace

Kiaya

Indira

Harry

Jake

Lucy

Freya

 **XTENSION**

Write the names of 12 children in your class in alphabetical order.

Copy these patterns into your book.

ᒻᒻᒻ ᒻᒻᒻ ᒻᒻᒻ ᒻᒻᒻ

ᑎᒷᑎᒷ ᑎᒷᑎᒷ ᑎᒷᑎᒷ ᑎᒷᑎᒷ

ᵒᵒᵒ ᵒᵒᵒ ᵒᵒᵒ ᵒᵒᵒ

rere rere rere rere

vv vv vv vv

lolo lolo lolo lolo

Copy these words into your book.

lid	dig	sing	ding
the	them	still	stilts
are	there	moon	room
growl	prowl	off	flood

EXTENSION

A Copy these sentences into your book.

A quick brown fox jumps over the lazy dog.

The five boxing lizards jumped quickly into the water.

B What do you notice about the sentences in **A** above?